Hysteria 11

Winning short stories, flash fiction and poems from the
Hysteria 2025 Writing Competition

Edited by Linda Parkinson-Hardman

Hysteria 11

Copyright ©2025, Linda Parkinson-Hardman

All rights reserved. The right of the individual contributors to be identified as the author of their work has been asserted in accordance with the Copyright, Designs and Patents Act 1988.

No paragraph of this publication may be reproduced, copied or transmitted save with written permission or in accordance with the provisions of the Copyright, Designs and Patents Act 1988, or under the terms of any license, permitting limited copying issued by the Copyright Licensing Agency, 33 Alfred Place, London, WC1E 7DP.

Any person who does any unauthorised act in relation to this publication may be liable to criminal prosecution and civil claims for damages.

Published by: Crystal Clear Books

ISBN: 978-1-0684474-6-4

Website: www.hysteriawc.co.uk

All characters in this publication are fictitious and any resemblance to real persons, living or dead is purely coincidental.

Cover Image: zarelyafr from Pixabay

ABOUT THE HYSTERIA WRITING COMPETITION

Hysteria is an (almost) annual, international writing competition opening in Spring and ending, this year, on 30th June. You can find out more about the competition, including rules and guidelines for entries on the website: *www.hysteriawc.co.uk*.

Dedication

The competition, and this anthology, wouldn't be possible without the support and help of a wonderful team of readers and this year's writer in residence:

Charlotte Emery, Daphne Larner, Eithne Cullen, Sally Anderson, Dianne Bown Wilson, Patricia Good, Pilar García Claramonte, Rachel Angel, Chris Muscato, Annette Iles, Sue Spiers, Heather Cook, Maureen Abel, Steven Patchett, Yvonne James, Denarri Peters, Abigail Ottley

You can meet this years readers on the website here:
https://hysteriawc.co.uk/hysteria-readers-2025/

Foreword

I am very fond of the Hysteria Writing Competition, not least because it forces me to confront the reality of a life spent with words. Each of the pieces in this year's anthology is a testament to the time taken to craft an image that implants an idea into the reader's head.

Every single one is different, and yet they all tell the same story, one that has an unbroken lineage over thousands of years, and that is the story of what it is to be human.

We can only ever 'write what we know'; yet it's impossible write what we don't, yet that piece of advice is often given as an admonishment to those who practice the craft as an attempt to keep them in a box labelled with their specific specialty or knowledge. These stories and poems demonstrate that the box cannot be closed forever, it cannot be tied shut and the ideas kept sealed, hidden. Instead, they flow freely through the minds and imaginations of everyone who contributes to this book.

I would like to offer my thanks to everyone who participated, just because you are not featured in these pages does not mean your entries were not worthy and I hope you will continue to write, to share your box of delights with readers and competitions alike.

Linda

Contents

ABOUT THE HYSTERIA WRITING COMPETITION 3
FOREWORD 4
READERS ADVICE TO ENTRANTS 7
FLASH FICTION 10
HOPING THE FIGHTING TEMERAIRE WILL HELL HIM SLEEP 11
THE BEAUTY OF MATHS 13
SPRING DREAMS, AUTUMN FOLLY 14
WHAT HAPPENS IF YOU KEEP THE CAMERA ROLLING AFTER THE FIRST KISS 16
LEVELLING UP DOWN TOWN 18
ALL THE THANKS I NEVER OFFERED 20
OH I DO LIKE TO BE BESIDE THE SEASIDE 21
FROM LAW TO WAR 23
CUBICLE 4 25
DADAJI'S BUCKET LIST 27
POETRY 28
ENCHANTED FAIRGROUNDS 29
A PRESSING PROBLEM 31
PERSPECTIVE 32
BARBIE DOLL 33
GLOSSY IBIS 34
MEETING A FRIEND 35
MRS EDWARDS IS AT HOME 36
MOTHER NURTURE 37
HUSH 38

ROCK BOTTOM	39
SHORT STORIES	41
POR UNA CABEZA	42
LAUGH TRACKS	45
PEOPLE, RAIN AND STREET JAZZ	49
15 HOUR BRIDE	52
YOUR CALL	56
SEABEAST	58
SHEDDING	62
CONSUMED	66
REACHING HOME	69
WHEN HARRY MET SALLY	73

READERS ADVICE TO ENTRANTS

The Hysteria Writing Competition is supported by a team of volunteer readers for each category. They read and assess each entry based on a common set of guidelines. They are often writers in their own right, many have won awards and competitions, and between them they bring a wealth of experience about what works and what doesn't. Each year I ask if they would like to share some feedback about how to enter competitions, common pitfalls and problem areas. Below is a selection of the advice I've received this year.

You can remind yourself of the reading team on the website here: hysteriawc.co.uk/hysteria-readers-2025/

Readers Advice from Heather Cook

1. Repetition - either of a pet phrase or a slightly unusual word - is particularly noticeable in a short story/poem and sticks in the reader's mind. Repetition has to serve a very clear purpose if used, convincing the reader that the writer understands their craft.
2. Nothing is more disappointing to a reader than feeling that the writer's energy has flagged part way through. The author may be convinced that they have a final twist which will knock the reader's socks off, but it is vital to maintain interest and tension until the last full stop.
3. Not an original thought, but spelling, punctuation, grammar!! Readers like to feel that writers care about their work and about what their readers think.

Readers Advice from Denarii Peters

As a reader, I look for a strong beginning. It may be a cliché, but it's still true: if your first line doesn't grab, it's an uphill struggle for attention.

In a short story, the middle should be concise: no waffling on about how pretty the countryside is and how amazing the buildings. Characters matter, but plot matters more.

The best short stories are not written in a day, although they may be plotted in an hour. That's when the real work starts. Edit, edit and edit again. Check for tension. Look at word choices and eliminate any repetition.

Make your ending as strong as your beginning, preferably with a bit of a twist.

And if you manage all that, you'll be an author worthy of the name.

Readers Advice from Sue Spiers

Some advice on writing poetry I adopt is to read widely, possibly anthologies from poetry presses (libraries tend to only stock dead poets' work) which will give you an idea of different approaches to writing in both subjects and presentation. If you hope your poem will get into the Hysteria anthology, earlier issues of the anthology are a good place to start.

Here are some pieces of advice that I've gleaned over the years and can share with you: Prose is like a river flowing the words in a stream, Poetry is like a fountain making patterns and arcs; A process for poetry is to ARRANGE the structure, DEEPEN the meaning and ENCHANT your reader. And finally, researching the theme or subject of a competition can lead you to interesting stories and a wider vocabulary of specialist words which, used sparingly and with hints at meaning energise poetry.

Readers Advice from Chris Muscato

Flash fiction can be tricky, and that's all part of the fun. Here's some of the things I've found (as a writer and a reader) that tend to make flash fiction successful.

First, consider the pacing. You don't have too many words to work with, so the story needs to keep moving. A little exposition that slows down a novel is often fine. In flash fiction, it can stop the narrative in its tracks, without leaving enough room to regain momentum. The reader does not need to know everything, and in fact one of the joys of flash fiction is playing with the balance of known/unknown. In this sense, don't be afraid of negative space.

Next, when writing, try to tell your story as simply as possible. I'm talking elevator-pitch levels of simplicity. This will not be the final version of your story, you'll fill it out with more details and some beautiful prose, but it really helps to know what needs to be said. What are the crucial elements of this story, and how can you communicate that efficiently? Personally, I start almost every work of flash fiction as a poem. I'm not a very good poet, but the mindset required to compress something into a poem helps me think about the central ideas, themes, and literary motifs that I'm building the story around. Then I take the poem and expand it into prose.

Finally, avoid overly dramatic twist endings. I understand why they're popular, and tempting to write into flash fiction. And, to be fair, they can be done really well. But more often than not, the twists I see in submissions feel like an attempt to wrangle meaning out of a story through shock more than consistency. If a theme or idea is central to the understanding of your piece, build it into the narrative. Don't save it for a dramatic twist at the end.

Readers Advice from Patricia Good

I thought this year's entries to the Flash Fiction category of the competition were of a high standard and I enjoyed reading them.
The entries that stood out for me were those that used clever and original imagery and those that satisfied with a complete story. A few entries, however well-written, were more of an anecdote than a complete narrative.
As the word count is limited in Flash Fiction the writing can't rely too much on lengthy back story or explanations. A piece of advice I follow is to begin as close to the action as possible, perhaps in the middle or at the point of conflict.
Another tip I use is to read or listen to my work being read out loud. This ensures I pick up on punctuation errors, repetitions or overused phrases and can hear how the work flows.
If possible leave your work aside for a while as re-reading it at a later date can highlight weak points.
Finally, it's not always easy to share our work with others so thanks for the opportunity to do so in this year's Hysteria competition.

FLASH FICTION

The Flash Fiction category is open to entries with a maximum word count of 250 words. These ultra-short stories need to be complete and give the reader the satisfaction of not being left hanging.

Despite its extreme brevity it should still offers the author and reader the benefit of character and plot development.

The overall category winner for the Flash Fiction category is 'Spring Dream, Autumn Folly' by Denarii Peters.

Hoping The Fighting Temeraire Will Hell Him Sleep

BD Watson

At 5.25 on a dark gloomy day Ernest McLintock is sitting on a bench in the gallery staring at the painting of the Fighting Temeraire by Turner.

He's incompetently eating coleslaw with a teaspoon, bits falling into his lap.

Maisie had made him promise he'd eat his greens on his last visit to the hospice.

He is closing and opening his eyes rhythmically trying to take a mental photograph of the painting that he can retrieve later.

It was her cure for insomnia.

"Just stare into the darkness, pictures appear, and you'll drift off." she would say while patting his arm.

A month from losing her, it's just not working.

Ernest is making a mess. He is using his eyes like a camera shutter, munching open-mouthed.

A skinny boy is standing mimicking Ernest's eye tic.

"Hey" shouts the servitor, "no food to be eaten here."

"What ARE you doing " says the youngster as Ernest sheepishly puts the pot of coleslaw into a plastic bag and rolls the top closed.

"Em," he coughs not knowing how to explain, "I'm trying to take a picture with my eyes." He demonstrates again.

The youngster scrabbles around in his baggy jeans pocket and pulls out a state of the art iPhone.

"Use this and I'll send you a copy to your email address" he smiles earnestly.

"That's so kind of you. Can you send it to my wife's email? She was better at all that than me."

B D retired in April 2021 from a content design job writing for advisers about peoples' rights . She's spent so much time with words she thought she would try to be creative with them. She joined Writers HQ and started to learn about writing. She tries to write every week on the Flash Forum on that site. It's a great learning community. She's also learnt a lot from Joe Gatford and Matt Kendrick. She's had work published in Pure Slush volumes and Trash Cat lit website. She lives in Edinburgh and writes from a table that looks onto the Pentlands.

THE BEAUTY OF MATHS

Chris Cottom

Suppose your father hadn't been a Cold War diplomat, hadn't been posted to the sleepy spa town of Baden-Baden on the slopes of the northern Black Forest. Suppose Annaliese Müller hadn't let you walk her home every afternoon after school, her eyes sparkling as she babbled about algebra and arithmetic, about what she called the 'beauty of maths'. What if, there in the sunshine on the banks of the Oosbach, she hadn't slipped her arms around your neck, made you count to ten in German, made you do it again backwards, before at last letting you kiss her?

What if, at the end of summer, your father hadn't been moved yet again, consigning you to a four-year stretch at a dank Yorkshire boarding school and the prospect of certain failure at an exam called, with grim irony, Elementary Maths? Let's say you hadn't remained pen friends with Annaliese throughout your teens, her letters full of fractions and formulae, yours with anecdotes and incidentals, never mentioning how you felt, how much you missed her.

Suppose at sixty-six and single, struggling with the mathematical conundrum of how many years you might have left, you picture Annaliese at her desk in that dusty Baden-Baden classroom, her fingers flying over the beads of her abacus. Suppose you take a motoring holiday around Baden-Württemberg, suppose you knock on her door. What if, also single, Annaliese were to find the formula to start over again, on a sunny afternoon on the banks of the Oosbach?

Chris Cottom lives near Macclesfield, UK. He's packed Christmas hampers in a Harrods basement, sold airtime for Radio Luxembourg, and served a twelve-year stretch as an insurance copywriter. He liked the writing job best.

chriscottom.wixsite.com/chriscottom

Spring Dreams, Autumn Folly

Denarii Peters

Tethered, fluttering green, the leaves are caught in a mid-spring dream.

The round, fat robin teases: "See me fly, go where I will."

"One day, we too will be free; the twig will release us. Only patience is required. For now, we serve the tree. But it promises a great reward will soon be ours."

The oldest leaf listens as the wind whispers, "You are right, and I will wait for you until the seasons turn. Then what games we will play, you and I!"

Brown sparrow, three summers wise, nesting high, grateful for the shelter of the leaves: "Do not wish your time away. Freedom is not the change you should seek. First find out how the tree will repay the work you do."

The branches creak, drowning out the sparrow's chirp. They would rather the leaves knew nothing of their fate.

The work of three seasons is all the tree requires. Then, as autumn ends the summer's smile, the leaves, now useless, as with their predecessors and those who will come after, will be persuaded to depart.

But it is only a pretence of setting free. In their gowns of bright, new colours, they rustle as the complicit wind shakes the weakening boughs.

"We go to see the world. Farewell, oh tyrant tree!"

But a single wing never carried anyone aloft and, cascading down, the oldest leaf realises the words of those who make use of you are always honeyed lies.

Flying, floating, drifting, dying.

Dead.

Prizewinning author Denarii Peters was born in the north-west of England but is now lost in the Lincolnshire Wolds. A former primary school teacher, she now spends her days writing stories and drinking a lot of coffee. In recent years, she has achieved longlist or better in more than seventy-five competitions, resulting in over twenty of her pieces being published in various anthologies. As a result of winning the short story prize for Hysteria in 2023, a collection of her work, Will You Walk into My Parlour, was published by Crystal Clear Books in October 2024. Her debut novel, The Reluctant Reaper, the first of a trilogy, appeared in July 2025, with the sequels scheduled for the new year.

denariipeters.substack.com

What Happens If You Keep The Camera Rolling After The First Kiss

Laura Besley

ACT ONE: Pre-production
We pretend we're each other's firsts. Your hands, your lips, laying claim to every part of me.

'I've never felt this way before,' you whispered.

I watch the globules of your lava lamp bop up and down. I believed you. I told you I felt the same.

ACT TWO: Standby
I grew up in the 1980s when women were whistled at, wore shoulder pads and had big hair.

In romcoms, no matter how hard the struggle, they always kissed at the very end.

Arguing over too little money and too much drinking doesn't seem very Hollywood.

ACT THREE: Action
On Sunday mornings, you watch the kids while I go supermarket shopping. It's like a time out. In the queue, a stranger plucks a leaf from my hair, a gesture so intimate, I blush. That night, I think of him, and touch myself, you sleep beside me.

ACT FOUR: Cut
We used to send text messages from work:
    Thinking of you! Can't wait to see you!
    Now, our WhatsApp exchange is filled with things like:
    It's your turn to pick up the kids.
    OK.
    Did you finish the milk?

Yes. Sorry.
Going to be late.
Again?

ACT FIVE: Post-production
Sometimes I wonder what happened to those romcom couples after they kissed. Did they stay together? No-one makes films about those lives.
    Or our life.
    Is there still reel in the canister? Does our script still have scenes to play out? Or is this a wrap?

Laura Besley writes short and very short fiction and enjoys exploring big topics in small spaces. She has published four collections, most recently: Sum of her PARTS (V. Press). She is currently a Creative Writing PhD student at the University of Leicester, an editor with Flash Fiction Magazine and runs The NIFTY Book Club. Having lived in the Netherlands, Germany and Hong Kong, she now lives in land-locked central England and misses the sea.

www.laurabesley.com

LEVELLING UP DOWN TOWN

Lee Irving

An old man sits on the street clutching a small box. By his feet stands a homemade sign, which reads:

FOR SALE
Octogenarian's dentures
1 careful owner

'Whose are they?' asks a man in a sharp suit.
   'Mine,' says the old man.
   'Why are you selling them?' asks the other man, putting a leather briefcase down by his feet.
   'I'm hungry.'
   'How can you eat without any teeth?'
   The old man shrugs and sucks his gums.
   'How much do you want for them?'
   'Five pounds?' says the old man, eyebrows raised.
   The man in the sharp suit hands over a banknote, picks up his briefcase and turns to leave.
   'You forgot your teeth,' says the old man, holding out the box and adding, 'I'm not a beggar.'
   The man in the sharp suit turns back. He hesitates a moment, before grabbing the box from the old man and marching away.

Next morning, Sharp Suit has taken the old man's place, but there is no homemade sign.
   'What's in the box?' asks the old man.
   'Some old bloke's teeth,' says Sharp Suit.
   'How much do you want for them?' asks the old man.
   'Five pence.'

The old man searches through the pockets of his shabby overcoat until he finds a coin.

Sharp Suit takes his money and hands him back the box. 'Nice doing business with you,' he says.

'Much obliged,' says the old man, his eyes brimming with tears.

Born in North Yorkshire, Lee Irving now lives in Abingdon, Oxfordshire. A former History teacher, he currently works at the Ashmolean Museum and he volunteers for a local environmental charity. Lee writes to try to make sense of the world by exploring what it means to be human, and his work includes everything from micro-fiction to novels, for both adults and children. He has won a dialogue-only competition in Writing Magazine and he is a two-time winner of Tortive Lit's #FlashFiction101 competition. Lee's story Ticket to Ride will be published by F(r)iction magazine in 2026, and he has also been published by The Anansi Archive and Michael Terence Publishing. He has been longlisted for the Yeovil Literary Novel Prize on two occasions.

All The Thanks I Never Offered

Lindy Newns

You knitted me bright coloured sweaters for birthday after birthday, and sometimes for Christmas too,

"Come on," you'd say, "you look like you're off to a funeral. Let's have a smile!"

So bloody jolly. I gave the one in scarlet and blue to the charity shop. It was too big, so I had an excuse. The rest all went into the drawer under my bed. I couldn't bring myself to give them away, but never wore them. I never thanked you properly and they must have taken you ages to do. Hours sitting in front of the television, click clicking away.

The week after, it hit me. Stupid, but I wailed like a baby, thinking I'd never get another hand knitted sweater from my auntie. It was ungrateful of me not to have worn any of those jumpers you'd laboured over; I wanted to make up for it. I wanted warm memories in bright wool next to my skin.

I opened the drawer. A moth flew up and I just knew. I took the sweaters out one by one. There were tiny larvae burrowed into knit and purl. Fragments of lacy white chrysalides and everywhere, a scattering of holes and nibbled wool.

There was one I remembered – a matador jacket - cubes of scarlet, bright yellow, pink and turquoise. There were large holes in the back, and a scattering of tiny ones across the sleeves, but I put it on anyhow.

I'm wearing it now. It's beautiful. Thank you.

Lindy Newns regularly hosts Mostly Manchester Stanza group. Her poetry and flash fiction has appeared in Orbis, Acumen, Riggwelter, L'Ephemere, Popshot, and anthologies including Poems for Grenfell and she is a regular reader at various open mics in and around Manchester.

facebook.com/lindy.newns/

OH I DO LIKE TO BE BESIDE THE SEASIDE

Peter Wright

"Tell me, Dave, what's the most wonderful thing that could happen to you?"

"How do you mean, 'wonderful'?"

"You know, the bestest thing ever."

"I'm not sure. Perhaps a big win on the lottery or the gee-gees?"

"Is money all you can think about? Isn't there something more spiritual, such as happiness or wellbeing?"

"You've been on one of those new-age, namby-pamby, tree-hugging websites again, haven't you?"

"What if I have?"

Mary's always into some new fad or other, making my life a financial misery by what she calls "investing a little" (meaning, a lot) in the latest thing.

"So, how would you answer that question?"

"Well, I'd really like to relive my most perfect day all over again."

"Oh, yes? So, when was that?"

She grabs my hand. "Don't you remember, darling? We were on holiday in Blackpool; all afternoon at the Pleasure Beach, going on every ride. Then fish and chips on our way back to the hotel. Oh, Dave, such a lovely day: so warm, the birds singing; strolling along the prom, the tide swishing in, trams trundling along, the sun setting over the sea… Everything was wonderful. Wonderful!

"And that night, you were so… passionate. It had to be the best. You must remember. Don't you agree it was the most perfect day ever?"

"I'm not so sure. It may have been the most perfect day as far as you're concerned, but for me…

"I've never been to Blackpool in my life!"

Peter was born and raised in Lancashire, spent most of his working life as a chartered accountant in West Yorkshire and has recently retired to a small market town in Lincolnshire. He has been a member of various local creative writers' groups for some years but, apart from a few poems, one of which was published in 2024, has never entered a (prose) writing competition. Until now. Married for more years than he cares to remember to prizewinning writer Denarii Peters, he spends a lot of his time in the role of personal assistant and general factotum. Some of the creativity in the air must have rubbed off!

From Law To War

Russell Lloyd

I handled the door open and started in saying words I wasn't listening to. A distraction, theirs, not mine. Mine was in my hand, all blue-black sheeny blunt-nosed double-chambered metal.

"Who are...," asked the first of the four.

I raised my answer waist high and my arm rocked back in a rhythm, four times was enough.

Cordite hazed my view. I stood feet flat to the floor, legs stiff and took inventory.

"Why...," said the last of them.

I didn't have to deny him an answer, that word had been the last of him.

No way, you say, to treat upright citizens. Well, they hadn't been and they weren't now. I eased through the haze and bodies, didn't notice the décor much and left. At the door, I kicked over the stove and its coals, just for wickedness; they were going to burn here as well as the next life.

The alarms and sprinklers sounded rear of me. I nodded, moved on and outside. There was more to do.

On foot in the street, the tarmacadam, basted in the heat of the day, gave way a little under pressure, like I never had.

"Evenin', George," I said, fast lips spitting faster words from a mind that was no welcome at all.

George, on patrol on his usual beat with his elsewhere face and eyes empty of all they saw, gave me a nearly smile and a twitch of his nightstick.

I heard him say, "Goodnight, Detective."

In addition to amateur writer I have been a postman, clerk, frozen warehouseman, (all student days), solicitor, Army officer, life class model, medication information leaflet evaluator, TV extra, invigilator, mystery shopper, Quaker Warden, charity Secretary, rescue cat carer and cat chef. I started writing, found it cathartic, I have laughed and cried.

And if folks can find in the reading of it half what I discovered in the writing of it, they 'll laugh too and, yes, ooze a tear or three. Looking forward to a time when I can walk without arriving, think without deciding, change without aging, wait without counting, love without hurting and maybe in those aims my writing is my GPS and compass. In the meantime…I can be too busy, but I'm slowing down as fast as I can. Struggle with tech, bit of a Technosaurus Rex, miss my quill.

www.facebook.com/share/1FBDRrAzz7/

CUBICLE 4

Sadie Fleming

"Joshua, are you in there?"

I stop dead.

"Josh?"

"Mum?"

"Ah, I thought it was you."

My heart pounds. Isn't this the men's changing room?

"How did you know I was here?"

"I can see your jacket under the door."

Pointlessly, I kick it away. "No, I mean here, in this store?"

She mumbles something.

"I thought you and Auntie Mel were going to Primark." I try to sound casual.

"Oh, the queues were awful. What are you trying on, Darling?"

"Me? Oh, er... a suit. For interviews and stuff."

I can get out of this, I just need to divert her. But then another voice. Oh God, the Overbearing One.

"Have you found him, Sheila?"

"He's in here. Cubicle 4. He's trying on a suit."

"Ooh Josh, let's see. I bet you look like Colin Firth in that Kingsman film."

"No! I mean, it... it's too small."

"I'll get you a bigger size, love. Pop it under the door."

"No need. I don't like the style anyway. Why don't we catch up in the cafe?"

"But we've not long had lunch," Mum's voice again.

"Could you order me a latte? I'll be two minutes, max."

They head off toward the elevators, chatting.

I stare at my reflection.

What was I thinking? I look ridiculous. The waist is too high, and the armholes are tight, even with my skinny frame. And I have nothing – literally nothing – to fill it out up top.

Such a shame. It's a beautiful dress.

Sadie Fleming is an accounts administrator living in Sussex, but outside of working hours loves writing short stories, and has been lucky enough to have had several of them published online and in magazines. Having grown up reading the likes of Edgar Allan Poe, Ray Bradbury and Roald Dahl, it's not surprising that she is drawn to horror, dark humour and speculative fiction, but when it comes to competitions she embraces the challenge of trying her hand at any genre (although she can't guarantee that one of her characters won't eventually end up under the patio). She is currently in the drafting stage of her first attempt at a novel, and is extremely grateful to all the wonderful people in the writing community who generously offer encouragement and advice to novice writers like herself.

www.instagram.com/lazywritersadie

Dadaji's Bucket List

Taria Karillion

"Okay, time to leave base camp, Grandad."

Samir scrubbed the ice off his moustache with a paw-like glove and gazed at the panorama of sparkling white. A low whistle escaped his blue-tinged lips. "You and your bucket list - I can't believe you talked me into this... But I'm glad you did."

Crunching his way over to a way marker, he pulled out a bundle of black rods from his pocket. They sprang outward in a sudden, spindly bloom, forming a tripod. "...And no, this isn't for 'that ruddy Facebook', it's for the wall at home. Nani insisted!"

A fumble with his rucksack produced a small, tin box that he gingerly placed on the way marker, then tugged out his phone and set it atop the tripod with a magnetic snap-p-p.

"Hey Siri!" he dropped to his knees, calling over the blustering wind that was toying with swirls of fresh powder, "set the camera timer - ten seconds!"

Then, in a much softer voice, as he leaned forward and gently touched the box and then touched his forehead. "Charan sparsh, Dadaji...charan sparsh." The phone camera clicked, and Samir struggled to his feet, putting the box safely away again. "Right... " he squinted at the cloud-crowned summit, "let's get going before the weather closes in. We've not come this far to give up now, eh, Grandad?"

As he patted his rucksack then heaved at the straps, the dull, tinny rumble of the urn inside sounded uncannily like a chuckle.

POETRY

The poetry category sought entries with a maximum of 16 lines, not including spaces or the title. Many of our entries followed a strict rule of either four or five-line stanzas, but a few challenged this convention.

Poetry is a piece of writing in which the expression of feelings and ideas is given intensity by particular attention to diction (sometimes involving rhyme), rhythm, and imagery.

The overall category winner for the Poetry category is 'Mother Nurture' by Iain McGrath.

ENCHANTED FAIRGROUNDS

AC Clarke

'a nauseating article, which dwelt upon the "enchantment" and the "mystery" of circus and fairground; of "gypsy" encampments and other such "liminal" spaces Fran Lock 'White/Other'

Enchantment is the bearded lady
monetising her difference because what else?

Mystery is the elephant man
in a tent of sacking and sawdust proffering

a medical condition for a sixpenny view.
Liminal is the tent-flap into

a world of difference, grease-paint clowns,
nervy balancing acts, drugged lions,

the crack of the ringmaster's whip.
It's soon time up, time to move on

churned grass the only witness
till the rollers come out to smooth things over.

A C Clarke has published six poetry collections and six pamphlets, two in collaboration. 'A Natural Curiosity' was shortlisted for the Callum Macdonald Memorial Award. She was one of four winners in the Cinnamon Press 2017 pamphlet competition with 'War Baby' and was commended in the 2005 National Poetry Competition, and longlisted in the same competition in 2014. She has twice won the Second Light long poem competition. Her latest collection, 'Alive Among Dead Stars', was published by Broken Sleep Books last year ,A third collaborative pamphlet with Maggie Rabatski and the late Sheila Templeton is due out from Seahorse Publications in October. She lives in Glasgow.

www.scottishbooktrust.com/authors/a-c-clarke.

A Pressing Problem

Ann Gibson

She doesn't do fast fashion,
wears natural fibres washed
as little as possible in full loads at 30;
line-dried and worn into the ground.

She's stopped in her planetary tracks
to learn the heavy impression
ironing leaves on her footprint.

Hot under her crisp cotton collar and
smoothed linen trousers she's unsure
she can face the world unkempt.
But needs must, she has a go.

Conscious of every random ruck,
she squirms, tries to kid herself
she's sashaying crumpled eco-chic.

Uncomfortable, more penance than pride,
this might just be a carbon step too far.

> Ann Gibson spent her childhood in Dublin and now lives in North Yorkshire, UK. She has an MA in Literature Studies from York St. John University, studied in evening classes. She has published poetry in Acumen, Dream Catcher, Orbis, Prole, Obsessed with Pipework, Dreich and The Poets' Republic magazines as well as various anthologies. Her poetry has also appeared online in The High Window, Lighten Up Online, Snakeskin, Pulsar, Ofi Press Magazine, Toasted Cheese and The Ekphrasis Review.

Perspective

Anne Babbs

The radiographer was proud of her machine.
'Look how big this MRI is. How much room you'll have to lie still in?'
'Hmmm' I said.
Thinking how small the MRI was. How constrictive it would be.
I guess it's all a matter of perspective.

The radiographer was proud of her machine
'It's not as loud as the older MRI but have some ear buds just the same.'
'Hmmm' I said again.
Thinking how it didn't matter that the old one was louder.
This one was loud enough.
I guess it's all a matter of perspective.

I glided in. My head encased to save it moving.
The noises too loud. The space too small.
The future decided on the pictures.
I guess it's all a matter of perspective.

Anne Babbs is a poet based in the Black Country, which is part of the West Midlands. She has previously been published by Offa's Press and in Culture Matters. Anne is a disabled writer, who lives with the chronic illness Multiple Sclerosis and also has osteo-arthritis, both of which, inform some of her writing.

instagram.com/anne.babbs/

BARBIE DOLL

Christine Griffin

Tonight as midnight strikes
she will discard her silken slippers,
slash the satin negligee to pieces
throw the thong into the bin.

For the last time she will begin the ritual
sponging, patting, brushing, creaming
while he sleeps.

Tomorrow she will not get up at six
to re-create the Barbie doll he fell in love with.
When he wakes, she will turn to him
dishevelled, lined, puffy,
smelling of sweat and sleep.

'Look at me,' she'll say. 'Look hard.
Tell me you still love me. Say it.'

Christine writes poetry and short fiction and is widely published including in Acumen, Writing Magazine, The Dawntreader and Poetry Super Highway. She has performed her work at the Cheltenham Literature Festival and the Cheltenham Poetry Festival and she regularly reads at open mics.

Glossy Ibis

Glen Wilson

I see them, dipping in the shallows at dusk,
their heads incline, beaks like bowed styli
scribe and beguile the refracted colours
as they repose on water. And this would be
a place for exile, to lay your stories on galingale
and bog pimpernel, to wait in turf and churchyard
for autumn lady's tresses. Slivers of iridescence
cast off from each Ibis, light as thought. And then
they rise, following an ancient rumour, to leave
the bailiwick, to shed all tribal leases with the easy
thrust of a being in element. And I see a figure
across the bay, tear away from its own industry
and watch with me, as the flock flames on the horizon.

Glen Wilson is a multi-award winning and widely published Poet from Portadown. He won the Seamus Heaney Award for New Writing in 2017, the Jonathan Swift Creative Writing Award in 2018 and The Trim Poetry competition in 2019. He won the Padraic Fallon Poetry competition and Slipstream Open Poetry competition in 2021 and The Fosseway Writers Open Competition and These 3 Streams Poetry competition in 2022. He won the Poetry Kit Ekphrastic Poetry Competition in 2023. He won the Artemesia Arts Poetry Competition and Goldsmith Poetry Competition in 2024. His poetry collection An Experience on the Tongue is out now with Doire Press.

x.com/glenhswilson

Meeting A Friend

Heather Cook

She floats towards me,
bird face peeping from a nest of frosted twigs.
Robust in my mammalian vastness,
I cushion her chicken elbows,
imagine the snap of thread-like ribs.

Our day is gentled by her frailty,
colours washed by luminous air,
the tea shop scene a watercolour.
We reminisce and laugh,
but not the way we did, giggles welling
long after we'd forgotten what was funny.
When I go, I warm her sparrow hands
between my fleshy paws.
She is almost a spirit.

Heather has always enjoyed writing poetry and is delighted that retirement has given her more time to indulge this passion. She has been placed or shortlisted in various competitions, including Ware, Wildfire Words, Writing Magazine, Hysteria, Arundel and Vole. In 2023, she was joint winner of the Frosted Fire First pamphlet Award with her first collection, Out of the Ordinary. She is delighted to have completed her second poetry collection, Beware the Exploding Yogurt Pot, published by Crystal Clear Books in September 2025. Heather also writes about cats, contributing a quarterly article about the lighter side of life with felines to 'The Cat', the journal of the leading cat charity, Cats Protection.'

Substack @heathercook652159

Mrs Edwards Is At Home

Helen Kay

She is Mrs Noah, ark full of children
gazing out of the bedroom window.
Acres of grass wave in the breeze.

> Baddiley – once Badda leah – wood clearing.
> So many histories are buried here:
> Roman road, wars, medieval village.

Her wean's rib fingers grip, flash her back
to the groaning barque, a confetti of gulls,
the sea's grab and swoop, its sputum of salt.

> She smooths Walter's hair. Thoughts float – Gespenst
> How best to translate that – spectre, dead and vague,
> or hobgoblin, defender of the soil?

And how does she translate? Frau – woman
or wife? Next door her stepchild coughs, rasps, coughs,
already a ghost that spirits cannot save.

Helen Kay's debut collection 'It Was Never About the Kingfisher' (Dithering Chaps Press, 2025) was shortlisted for the 2025 Rubery Awards. Her work has appeared in many magazines including The Rialto, Butcher's Dog, Under the Radar, Poetry Society News and Interpreter's House. She was a finalist for the 2022 Brotherton Prize and won the Cheshire Prize for Poetry in 2024 and 2025. She is known on Facebook for her sidekick puppet influencer Nigella.

www.facebook.com/helen.kay2

MOTHER NURTURE

Iain McGrath

In making your family soup,
you treated thin skins with kid gloves,
tempering acerbic onions,
softening brittle carrots,
before leavening us with sliced leek and
an affection of lentils.

When we came to the boil,
with the patience of several saints,
you turned down the heat to cool,
nurturing your peppered, salty brood
to make us one.

Then, full of grace,
you gathered us in communion
around the family altar,
ladling your offering with seasonings of love,
and we broke bread together.

Iain McGrath is retired, and writing is his hobby. His first full length play 'Where There's a Will' was performed in 2025. He has had short stories published in Scribble and an Ireland's Own collection, and he won the Hammond House Publishing International Comedy Prize in 2022. Unaccountably, his mini musical 'Gordon Brown - The Musical' is still awaiting its premiere.

Hush

Kate Woodward

Don't talk about it. We know
the precious carving's clogged with dust
and the piano's a halftone off its pitch.
We know the billiard balls don't roll true,
the fish knives tarnish in a trice,
and our beads, buttons, collar studs turn yellow,
from white. Almost overnight.
Cursed perhaps, but in our house
it's not polite to own our guilt or raise regrets –
Tsk, tsk. Move on.
The elephant's in the room –
but we don't talk about it.

Kate Woodward is a freelance writer whose short stories have been published by Spelk Fiction, Brittle Star, The Ogham Stone and others. She has a Creative Writing MA and lives in rural Lancashire. Occasionally, she updates her website which can be found at:

kate-woodward.com

Rock Bottom

Simon Tindale

He poisoned her goldfish
She kidnapped his dog
He shattered her windows
She flooded his bog

He pissed on her doorstep
She spat in his face
He smashed up her motor
She questioned his race

He battered her father
She hit on his wife
He bullied her children
She threatened his life

He flattened her cities
She burned down his trees
He melted her ice caps
She emptied his seas.

> Simon was born in Sunderland
> sold songs in South London
> found poetry in West Yorkshire
> he likes people
> who put others first
> and dislikes those
> who talk about themselves
> in the third person
> his poems are fictitious

and bear no resemblance
to actual poems
whether living or dead
he hopes you enjoy them.

SHORT STORIES

The short story category is for entries of up to 1000 words, not including the title. The short story genre is a staple of writing competitions and many writers will hone their skills in this medium before venturing into the world of longer fiction.

A short story is something that can be read in a single sitting. According to Wikipedia, the written short story emerged from the tradition of oral storytelling in the 17th century.

The overall category winner for the Short Story category is 'Seabeast' by Rachel Swabey.

Por Una Cabeza

Adele Evershed

I searched through old albums for that photo of us in that restaurant. I know it's there somewhere—pressed flat and aging like all your old hankies that I keep in my top drawer, though I never use them. Once, when someone asked me what I'd grab if my house were on fire, I said my photos. They seemed irreplaceable. Of course, we've moved on—all the things I used to run my fingers over—letters, books, skin—I now keep in the cloud.

Was it Barcelona or Madrid? I think it must have been Barcelona, in the Gothic Quarter. You'd read on TripAdvisor about a rooftop bar that offered lessons in Argentinian tango.

"No experience necessary," you told me, stroking an imaginary mustache like a Latin lover from a black-and-white movie. We found it tucked like a secret whisper between cathedral spires.

I giggled up the staircase, nervous to step so far outside my comfort zone. You took the stairs two at a time, as if rushing to meet a new version of yourself waiting there with a welcome drink in hand.

But when we emerged into the brightness of the bar, blinking like a pair of moles, you looked disappointed to find a few plastic chairs, an older couple, and a bartender with his shirt open to his navel. I think you would have turned on your heels, but all those British good manners your mother crammed into you acted like a corset, keeping you in place.

As we sat, you gestured with your eyebrows at the man wearing sandals with socks. He was exclaiming loudly, in a Southern American accent I recognized from too many movies:

"Geeze honey, I'm so happy we did this. It's just like a film set."

You bit your lip to stop yourself from sniggering, but I liked his puppy-dog enthusiasm. We ordered sangria, so full of fruit it seemed more dessert than cocktail. As I nibbled on a soggy piece of apple, you read out the next day's itinerary, written in your tiny, cramped handwriting. It always made me smile—

such a contrast to your body, loose-limbed and always taking up more than your allocated space.

When the tango dancers appeared, they looked like they'd raided Valentino's dressing-up box from the 1920s rather than the 2020s. The man was classically beautiful, with skin like a marbled David, arched eyebrows, and chiseled cheekbones you could hang your doubts on.

And even dressed like a box of cheap confectionery, he smoldered. As he doffed his sharp-edged hat, the American woman whooped, jiggling the still air.

He smiled—the kind of smile that puts its recipient in a spotlight—and I knew immediately he enjoyed being the object of many a tourist's fantasy.

His partner was as pale as frostbite, with a curl in the middle of her forehead, like a question mark. The familiar, mournful music started, and the man took hold of the woman's arm, as if she were a tantruming toddler, and pulled her to the side of the makeshift stage.

For the next five minutes, I was mesmerized; the shabby bar, the fruit salad cocktail, the stereotypical Americans—all forgotten. I felt my pulse jump to the violence of the drama.

A hurricane in heels.

When it was over, I snapped a photo as they held a pose, seemingly oblivious to their audience. Then you asked Sandal Man to take a picture of us with the blue, cloudless sky behind us.

I think I was wearing a sundress covered in watermelons and espadrilles. I can't remember what you wore, but you were smiling as if you'd just bitten into a fresh peach and the juice was running down your chin.

When we sat again, I spilled sangria down my dress, and you gave me one of your giant white handkerchiefs to mop it up. It smelled of cotton, time, cologne—home.

We never took the lesson. I said I felt a migraine coming on. As we left, the lady dancer told the American couple the tango was a walking dance, so anyone could do it. I knew that might be true, but anything I tried would be a frog trying to swim like a swan. Like so many things, I couldn't bear to try.

Back in the present, I turn the sticky pages and find the photo in a section labeled "Buenos Aires." I'm wearing a grey slip of a dress as soft as smoke, red strappy sandals, and a glass of champagne sweating on the table.

I'm looking up to where you should be, but there are only bruised clouds filling the sky.

Adele Evershed is a Welsh writer who swapped the Valleys for the American East Coast. Her work has appeared in Poetry Wales, Modern Haiku, The Ekphrastic Review, Atrium, and Literary Mama. Adele has two poetry collections, Turbulence in Small Spaces (Finishing Line Press) and The Brink of Silence (Bottlecap Press). Her third collection, In the Belly of the Wail, is forthcoming with Querencia Press. She has published two novellas-in-flash, Wannabe and Schooled (Alien Buddha Press), and has a third, A History of Hand Thrown Walls, forthcoming with Unsolicited Press. Her short story collection, Suffer/Rage, was recently released by Dark Myth Publications.

adeleevershed.com.

Laugh Tracks

Brandon Keaton

Megan Jones is six hours past the funeral, already rationing tissues because her mum—the thrift shop queen—disliked "single-use" anything. The bedroom smells of talc and scorched cinnamon; the windows slightly cracked, moths ricocheting off the glass like confused confetti.

She leans against a walnut chest of drawers—another relic bound for storage. The dresser scoots an inch, kicking up dust; she sneezes.

"Great," she sighs. "Grief and hay fever, the double feature nobody asked for."

She kicks at one of the dresser's claw feet. It rocks, sulky as a vending machine withholding some sweet treat.

CLANG.

A brass key, clothespin-sized, skitters across the hardwood floor.

Megan pockets the key like incriminating evidence. First stop: Mum's jewellery box... no luck. Underneath the box is a dog-eared notebook titled "Half-Baked Punchlines, M.J., Age 16." She cringes—ancient stage dreams, best left forgotten.

She tries the wardrobe: a roll of church raffle tickets, a dusting brush from the vacuum cleaner, and a receipt for a scented candle labelled Teenager Angst.

"Nothing says empty-nest like eau-de-teen."

Key still cold between her fingers, Megan eyes the ceiling hatch just outside the bedroom door. The attic ladder hasn't been deployed since she was twelve and convinced Gollum lived up there.

"Sneaky Hobbitses," she mutters, tugging the cord. A bare bulb flicks on, buzzing like a tired fridge.

Under her weight the ladder groans like it remembers every missed mortgage payment, but it holds. She climbs, heart pattering with the faint thrill of rule-breaking even though the only authority figure is six feet under—and probably cheering.

The attic air tastes of insulation and Christmases past. Boxes tower like loose chess pieces. She tries the key in a wicker toy-chest: padlock too fat, the key rattles around. Next, an old cash tin from Mum's online antique business: wrong shape.

She groans, wiping her brow. "Goldilocks meets Fort Knox."

Then she spots it: a decorative wooden lockbox, balanced on a beam the width of a paperback. Pink tape seals the box's edges—Mum's signature stationery.

Megan inches across a joist, gripping rafters for balance. The box teeter-totters, but she lifts it down intact. A golden keyhole guards the hinged lid, and—click—the key fits as if scripted.

Inside are a voice recorder, five mini-cassettes: each Sharpie-scrawled with their own title. Underneath, a glitter-splattered karaoke microphone, and a USB stick wrapped in a sticky note.

Her laugh comes out wrong—half amazement, half anger.

"Seriously? Were you open-mic Barbie?"

From somewhere downstairs, a clock strikes the hour, reminding her the world is continuing without either of them.

Megan pockets the USB and the mic, then slides Tape #1 into the handheld recorder she'd seen Mum use to tape her minister's favourite sermons with.

The play button clicks. Static crackles.

Mum's voice—alive, playfully conspiratorial—lights up the dark.

"Good evening, Athenian Sports Bar! I'm Natalie Jones—single mum, professional bargain-hunter. You can probably guess my love language. I call it 'Reduced to clear.'"

A ripple of audience laughter answers. Megan smirks despite herself.

"Oh, Lord... coupon humour."

Natalie segues into a riff about swiping right on profiles in her age group proclaiming "carpe diem," but upon meeting they proceed to drive in circles, refusing to pay for parking. The laughter swells—full-throated, rowdy.

Megan's eyes begin to sting. The tape clicks off mid-joke—Tape #2 already begging to be heard.

She rewinds just enough to hear the applause again; proof her mother once owned a room. She pockets the cassettes, then clambers back down the ladder.

In the kitchen, she opens her laptop, and slots the USB stick in. A single video file loads: openmic_final.mp4. Timestamp: two weeks before the cancer biopsy Mum swore was a routine check-up.

Megan hesitates—then hits play.

The screen frames a dimly lit makeshift stage, fairy lights sagging over a mic identical to the glitter-covered one in her pocket. Mum walks on, clutching note cards. No one claps. She starts anyway—voice thinner than the tape's confident thrum.

"They say laughter's the best medicine. Too bad my insurance doesn't cover hecklers."

Silence.

A glass clinks somewhere off camera.

Megan's stomach knots, but she can't look away.

Natalie soldiers through punch lines that flop like fish on carpet. Halfway in, she abandons the cards. Her smile wobbles.

"Tough crowd. Probably a good thing—if I get any laughs, they'll ask me to come back."

Megan finds herself muttering the tag line one beat ahead, muscle-memory from kitchen table rehearsals she'd long forgotten.

On-screen, Natalie exhales through pursed lips, then steps closer to the mic.

"Megan?" She pauses. "Kiddo, if you're watching this, finish the set for me, okay? Don't let the punchline die."

The video runs for three more seconds, Natalie grins from ear to ear—then it cuts to black.

Megan rewinds the cassette and presses play. Applause swells—clean, identical, a little too perfect. She scrubs back and counts the exact same whoop, the same off-key whistle, and the same handclap—again, again.

Then it clicks—it's a studio laugh-track with looped applause pasted over real silence.

The truth lands like an empty glass on tile.

Natalie hadn't basked in adoration; she'd imported it, patching together disappointment with her bedroom boombox the way she mended hems—cheap thread, steady hands, make-do faith.

Megan's throat tightens.

She tilts the glitter-spattered mic under the kitchen light.

Flecks fall like tiny comets.

"It's time," she murmurs, voice thick. "Let's trade canned for the real thing."

*

The Sticky-Wicket Comedy Club squats between a laundromat and a donut shop, windows fogged with last night's lager. A clipboard on the bar reads "Open-Mic, 7 p.m."

Megan's palms sweat as she prints M. Jones on the last blank line, the pen squeaking like it's rooting for her.

She slips Natalie's pocket recorder next to the glitter mic in her back pocket and flicks it off—no more borrowed applause.

Beyond the curtain, real laughter rolls.

"Okay, Mum. Here we go."

Brandon Keaton is the author of the award-winning novel Transference, an indie published sci-fi romp. His shorter work has seen print in Ironclad, Friction magazine, and most recently his tale about a sentient calculator published by SpecFicNZ won the 2025 Sir Julius Vogel Award for Best Short Story. Brandon lives in New Zealand where he continues — on a daily basis — to try and pull his own head from out of the clouds.

linktr.ee/keatonisbatman

People, Rain And Street Jazz

Glenn Holmes

Janine tried the bus shelter just as the rain started to spot but even if everybody 'moved right down' there wasn't even standing room. She made it into the shop doorway a hair's breadth before the real downpour. Five seconds later, he arrived, a newspaper over his head and looking decidedly bedraggled. He looked up and seemed surprised to see her.

"Erm, look, I'm sorry. I'll nip along the street and find somewhere else."

"Don't be daft, you'll get soaked. I'll budge up a bit. We'll both fit in, no problem," she replied." He was good looking enough to merit a smile. She gave him a smile.

"It's just that you read all this "me too" stuff nowadays. It's getting dark and I don't want to make you feel uncomfortable," he said

"You aren't auditioning me a film part just sheltering from the rain in a shop doorway." As promised, Janine budged up. "Get in before you drown me with drips".

He stepped into the doorway and ran a hand through his hair to brush out the excess rainwater. Janine got her share. "Oh no, I am sorry. That was really stupid of me."

"Don't worry, if that's the worst thing that happens to me today, it'll have been a good day."

"Has it? Been a good day?" he asked.

"I've been working late, and I'll have to make me own dinner when I get in so not so much good as typical." she replied. He smiled and they lapsed into silence. After a while, Janine said, "I quite like it when it's like this."

"Cold and wet?"

"No, quiet but noisy, Listen." A discarded cola bottle rattled in the gutter. "He's part of the glass wind section. He's just getting tuned up."

He smiled, "Glass wind, I like it"

"See that pile of newspapers in the newsagent's doorway opposite, the ones with the plastic ties on them." The wind caught the pile, and it riffled and seemed to moan. "They're Greek Chorus doing it's warming up exercises."

"For their gasps and heart rending sighs of longing in the second act?" he asked.

"You're getting the idea. Those parking restriction signs, the ones rattling on the lampposts, they're the other part of the percussion section."

"Part? Where's the rest?"

"Those dried up leaves trapped in the drainpipes. They're on the snare drums. You know, with those drumsticks that look like brushes. I don't know the proper name for them."

He grinned and said, "Drum brushes."

She gave a little laugh, "Well there's a surprise."

He smiled and said, "Those leaves, round here, they must be guest artists. You know, probably just blew in from out of town."

Janine groaned, "That was awful."

"It was, wasn't it. But you liked it."

"I did."

What do they play?" he asked

"Street Jazz. All improvised" she replied.

"See the way that the wind blows the rain across the road. When we were little, my brother used to call that people rain because he said it looked like people rushing across the road," he said.

"So, what do you reckon, they're scurrying across the road to get to their seats for the Street Jazz?"

"Either that or the rain's just hurrying to get in out of the rain." He pointed to a pair of polystyrene burger boxes lodged in a corner, locked in each other's embrace. "What about those two?"

"They've clicked. Burger boxes always pull. They're just waiting for the slow dance at the end so they can finally cop off" she answered.

They went quiet for a minute.

"My bus is due soon," he said. "The 311."

"I catch the 311," she replied.

"I know," he said. "I see you most mornings."

"You do, do you?"

"I get on two stops before you. Seems you've made more impression on me than I have on you."

She smiled and said, "Up to now, maybe. If the rain doesn't ease, we'll just have to make a dash for it."

"Don't worry," he said reaching into his coat pocket. "This'll keep off the worst". He produced a telescopic umbrella. She looked at him. "It isn't only Street Jazz that's improvised," he said.

"What if I hadn't budged up?" she asked.

"Who'd want to get to know a girl like that? I'd rather take my chances with the people rain."

She laughed. "I'm Janine."

"I'm Dan."

She smiled and linked her arm through his. "Maybe today isn't as typical as I thought. Okay, Dan, get that umbrella up and we can take our chances with the people rain together."

Glenn Holmes is a retired trainer of teachers who decided that having spent much of his working life asking others to write, he ought to do some himself. Originally from Liverpool, he feels growing up bombarded by Liverpudlian "wit" has been a huge help. He lives in London with his Slovakian wife and their fifteen year old daughter. Now he spends a good deal of time each year in Slovakia. His abject failure to master that language has renewed his love of English. He denies any suggestion that this pseudo patriotism marks him out as a scoundrel.

X.com/GlennHo97250326

15 Hour Bride

Julie Bailue

We'd only been married for fifteen hours when my beautiful wife left me forever, never to be seen again.

I was 20 years old and on a road trip with some college buddies. We'd been driving for a couple of days, stopping off here and there and anywhere. On one occasion, we went for a few beers at a bar in a town in Nevada. We placed our orders, and when mine was taken, time stood still, and my heart raced.

The waitress was a tiny Goddess, doll-like, with dark eyes and a fragile beauty that challenged you to resist her.

The afternoon slid into the evening, and soon my friends left to explore the city, and it was just me left nursing a drink and drowning in Lily Mae's soul.

"I finish at midnight," she said. "We go somewhere. Enjoy ourselves, yes?"

"Yes."

She sucked on a cigarette and blew smoke rings that circled above her like tiny halos on invisible angels.

I left the bar with my Cinderella and headed on to another. We drank cheap wine, followed up by tequila chasers, and I fell head over heels.

We talked into the night, she told me her plans, she wanted a white wedding and a house with a front garden and a back garden and the warm arms of a loving husband to welcome her into her Leave it to Beaver world.

I told her I was going to make a lot of money one day, run my own business, employ hundreds of people, and be somebody.

She smiled and nodded then. "Yes, you can do that, I know you can."

She laughed and twisted the chain on her pendant slowly and purposefully as though she was wrapping me around her little finger.

"Lilly Mae, that's a beautiful name."

"You think so? My mother named me after her friend, she die just before I was born, my mother says that when she die her spirit entered my soul and I became her."

She laughed out loud and ordered more drinks. The barman seemed to know her; she called him Jack, and he said, "You go easy there, Beverley."

"Beverley?" I spoke.

She cocked her head to one side and leaned into me, "Take no notice, I am Lily Mae, let's go somewhere else."

She waved at the bartender, and I swear he winked back at her. Off we went to continue this never-ending night. We found a basement bar down an alley off the main drag where we enjoyed fancy cocktails and munched on little sausages on sticks.

Before I could stop myself, the words gathered in my throat like demonstrators at a protest meeting, and when given the signal, unleashed their feelings boldly with emotion.

"Marry me, Lily Mae, right now, we'll find a place, then we can be together, live in a little house with a front garden and a back garden, what do you say?"

A huge grin formed, and her lovely face transformed into delight.

"Okay." She nodded.

I remembered what she said about wearing white,

'Stay here, I'll take care of everything."

I ran through the illuminated streets, a fairyland for grown-ups who should know better. I needed to hurry; if I stopped and took stock, the whole dream would end, fizzle out, and I'd be left trying to make sense of a miracle.

I stopped by a street stall and handed the Mexican trader twenty bucks for a little white summer dress. I picked up a ring, it had a plastic heart decorated with glitter stuck onto a plain gold band. I planned on getting something more traditional in the future, our future.

When I got back, she was still sat there, her teeny hand clutching the stem of the wine glass just as I'd left her, the cracked ashtray brimming with cigarette butts, she was so fragile and petite I feared she might fall into her drink and drown

We were married a few hours later at the Little Temple of Love Hearts in Las Vegas, with a couple of inebriated holidaymakers serving as our witnesses.

Only when I placed the cheap ring on her finger did I notice the tiny black lily tattooed on my bride's knuckle.

She smiled, "To remind me who I am," she said.

We booked into a motel across the road and began married life.

She was her namesake, a white petal unfolding to embrace the sun. We were floating before, just waiting to attach, and here we were now lovers, strangers, soulmates.

The next afternoon, after spending the whole of the first day of our married life together in bed, she announced she was going to get some ice.

I nodded and said, "Sure, don't be long." Then I lay back, reclining on the shabby double bed, glowing with achievement.

But she never came back, and when I checked my pockets, my wallet was also gone. Was this all some kind of bad joke that we'd laugh at over at our many anniversary dinners, surely not?

I waited all day, and even went back to the bar looking for her.

"Beverley?" asked the barman when I described my wife.

"Lily Mae," I said, "She's, my Lily Mae."

"Well, neither of them is working here anymore." He laughed a sad, knowing laugh and went to pour some other sucker a drink.

*

So, I did what was necessary to fulfil my legal obligation; I went back home, graduated, got married again after a lengthy engagement, and started a family. Now I'm an old man, my perspective has altered, I no longer live in hope, I accept my lot in life, I'm disappointed, I thought there would be more to it, in the end, I'm just a man like any other.

"Your coffee."

The surly waitress slops a chipped mug before me; her papery skin struggles to bind her old bones. The faint outline of a small black lily on her knuckle is just visible.

Julie started out writing as a child and won a playwriting competition at 13 with a piece set in a land in the clouds. When she came down to earth she studied drama and moved to London. After studying as an actress, she decided to write a stand-up routine and perform on the London comedy circuit, which she did for ten years, not with the same act. She has since written stage plays, radio plays, and sit-coms, short stories and articles for both print and online publications and anthologies. She has written the script for three musicals, one which had a successful national tour before a short West End run and has just completed a play about silent film star which she hopes to produce. She co-wrote stage plays and radio series with the comedienne Jenny Éclair for 15 years and has also just completed a 100,000 word Contemporary Gothic novel. She writes because her dreams at night are so vivid and magnificent and story led, that she figures if she can come up with all that when sleeping, perhaps she will achieve even more when awake.

YOUR CALL

J R Tucker

Midnight in the North Atlantic. A roaring south-westerly whipped the waves mercilessly as they towered and crashed against the colossal hull of the Resolute, clawing at her bow like a thing enraged. Captain Harrow stood braced at the helm, brow furrowed, eyes narrowed against the chaos as the black and white fury howled in the darkness like a beast denied.

The comms crackled into life - barely audible over the whining gyros and bursts of static.

'Cargo vessel, cargo vessel…. Please identify …. this is …. on emergency channel sixteen …. Please state your intentions …. dangerously close proximity…. Please alter course immediately. Repeat, please alter course immediately. Over."

Harrow snorted. "Who the hell do they think they are?" he muttered, grabbing the mic.

'Unidentified vessel, Unidentified vessel, this is The Resolute; ninety thousand tonnes of steel under international passage, a fully laden Panamax with two hundred souls aboard. YOU alter course. Over."

A pause. Then the voice returned, more firmly. "Cargo vessel Resolute …. it is imperative - repeat IMPERATIVE - that you alter your heading without delay – you are on a direct collision course with us…. Please confirm your diversion course NOW. Over."

Harrow's First Mate shifted uneasily.

"Sir? Navigational sensors aren't showing any large vessels and there's nothing of size scheduled in this lane. Maybe it's something small?"

Harrow's jaw tightened. "I will not be bossed about by some five-hand fishing boat! They can bloody well get out of our way!"

He jabbed at the mic again.

"Now listen here, whoever you are, this is The Resolute. We are a sovereign vessel under international maritime law. We do NOT yield. Over!"

Harrow give a brisk nod of 'put that in your pipe and smoke it, cheeky bugger', and turned to his First Mate, who uttered a wordless squeak as his eyes widened and he raised his arm, pointing out through the rain-battered wheelhouse window. Through the mist, a vast shape was emerging—tall, unyielding, impossibly close, and a single blinding beam of light pierced the night sky and illuminated the cabin for just a moment, causing both men to shield their eyes.

Harrow's face drained of colour, his mouth dropped open. And he let out a hoarse yell.

"ENGINES FULL REVERSE! HARD TO PORT! NOW, NOW, NOW!"

The radio crackled once more, then came,

'Resolute, be advised, we are categorically UNABLE to move - we are a LIGHTHOUSE!

... Your call!"

SEABEAST

Rachel Swabey

Maya bobs in the lizard-grey sea, just out of sight, as the gaggle of eccentrics, thrill-seekers and exhibitionists jostles on the pier, eager to leap towards glory. The serious-looking hang gliders have had their turn, so now it's time for the amateurs dressed as giant birds or vehicles. The wind whips at their costumes and contraptions, but they're all smiles and bravado.

A woman in a WWII spitfire costume launches herself from the ramp at the end of the pier and hangs in the air, a moment of elation containing within it the seeds of catastrophe. The freeze-frame spell breaks, and then so does the spitfire as the woman smacks into the ocean.

Lorna shoulders her way forwards, engineering a clear line-of-sight between herself and the local newspaper photographer in the dinghy below. The annual Birdman contest is always a double-page spread, often a front page picture too. Her white-feathered wings are as wide as she is tall and she's wearing a silver halo on a wire and a silver swimsuit. Because, of course, only an angel would throw herself off a pier for charity, right? Her skin is several shades darker than usual, making her blonde curls and white grin doubly dazzling. Maya can hardly bear to look, but she wants to see Lorna crash.

*

Maya started at Catalyst four months ago. Lorna, the only other female designer, had already been there four years. So perhaps it was a weird animalistic territory thing, or something. Who knows? Maya had long-since given up trying to second-guess Lorna's motives.

It was little things at first, like unplugging equipment at Maya's work station or moving her stuff, rattling her and making her doubt herself. By the time Maya figured out what was happening, the roles were set. Everyone had her pegged as the scatty one. To blame her screw ups on unflappable Lorna, who always made sure there was plausible deniability, would have seemed defensive, even ridiculous. It would have asked people to choose, and Maya was pretty sure how that would turn out.

At lunchtimes, Maya would head to the beach and eat a meal deal tuna sandwich with ready salted crisps, washed down with a lemonade. Then she'd strip to her swimsuit and tiptoe into the sea. Some days it felt like punishment, the sharp stones piercing her feet, icy waves nipping her ankles, but the sucking undertow always pulled her back and, by the time she was thigh-deep, bracing to launch into the surf, it always felt like freedom.

And when she was submerged, muscles aching, salt on her lips, the push-and-pull solitude and oneness of the sea, she felt as though she could let go of whatever Lorna's mind games had done to her nervous system that morning, as though the water leached it out of her somehow.

Afterwards, she would trudge back to the office to shower. Until the incident with her clothes. She couldn't prove Lorna took them, of course, but she knew straight away. And she had no choice but to stumble into the office in her towel and announce that her clothes had disappeared. The team of seven male designers sniggered and shuffled like eight-year-olds on a fire drill after Lorna and Maya into the ladies' changing room to help look for the missing changing bag. Lorna's face as Gary pulled it from under a bench – where it certainly hadn't been before – confirmed everything she had known as soon as she'd stepped out of the shower. Maya, still dripping, flushed and fought back tears.

After that, she dried under a changing robe at the beach.

"Oh, wow!" Lorna exclaimed one day, pulling seaweed from Maya's hair, holding it up like a prize as everyone gawped. "We'll have to start calling you Seabeast!" She cackled, to the usual chortling. Maya stared at the seaweed in Lorna's manicured hand. There was nothing she could say. She swallowed and it was as though she was swallowing something solid, as though a pebble was lodging itself deep in her gut, or some kind of anemone, sitting spiky within her, just waiting for an opportunity to sting.

*

Every evening in the shower, Maya watched sand swirl around the drain, barely noticing as day by day the skin on her legs began to take on a grey-green sheen. She scrubbed at it, but she couldn't seems to shift it. And besides, there was something strangely beautiful about its iridescence, especially in the water.

The colour deepened and spread, creeping up her torso, across her shoulders, up her neck.

"Are you quite well?" Lorna gasped when she noticed. "I hope you've been checking the sewage reports?" she added, nose wrinkling. "That can't be healthy."

Maya shrugged, saying nothing.

And she felt nothing either. It was as though the scorn ran off her more smoothly now, like water beading on her newly tough, slick skin.

When her skin began puckering into little lumps, she covered it with trousers and polo-necks. Perhaps she should have been more worried, but as her skin changed, it developed new sensations, as though her arms and legs could see, smell and taste everything they touched. It was intoxicating. The world became a riot of sensation. And swimming—swimming became particularly divine. She started going to the beach before and after work as well as at lunchtime.

*

On the pier, Lorna preens, enjoying her moment, if not in the sun then at least in the spotlight, then she takes her run-up and launches. Maya takes a second to enjoy the satisfying inelegance of Lorna's freeze-frame moment hanging above the sea, then sinks and propels herself towards the pier. She looks up at the silver swimsuit and sodden wings, and reaches a tentacle towards a flailing fake-tanned ankle. The leg jerks and Maya hears a distant scream that turns to a gurgle as she pulls Lorna under.

Above, a ray of refracted sunlight illuminates a floating halo of white feathers.

Rachel is a mother-of-three and regional newspaper subeditor from near Brighton, UK. She has won prizes for her short fiction and poetry with Anansi Archive, Globe Soup and the Steyning Festival Short Story Prize and her work has been featured in print anthologies from Fly on the Wall Press, Pure Slush and Mum Life Stories, and online at Punk Noir Magazine, Every Day Fiction and FlashFlood Journal, who nominated her for Best of the Net 2021. She's working on a novel, but can often be found bunking off with sneaky forays into poetry and short fiction. She is a big fan of Octavia Butler's writing, cheese (all varieties), and Richard Osman's House of Games.

www.threads.com/@spectopia

SHEDDING

Sally Curtis

"And you can take your devious hands off that!"

The woman from the council fled the museum as Arthur darted towards the stone pillar. Carved into its buttery-beige surface were two snakes, bodies and tails entwined, heads facing, tongues touching. His companion for thirty years, it gave Arthur a sense of security, steadfast in its silent presence. It didn't taunt him with spiteful gibes; didn't pledge to love him forever and then run off with his best friend of fifty years; didn't return from its shrewd sister's demanding a share of the house and half his pension before disappearing like a snake in the grass. No. His serpents could be trusted not to bring bad apples to the table.

Now everything was going to change again, but until then, Arthur was determined to stand guard, which was the opposite of Young Gerald who, firstly, was a pacer and secondly planned to move from his parent's house on his 40th birthday to the neighbouring village. Why people had to continually move about, Arthur couldn't fathom. Moving forward, moving on, and as for all this finding yourself – Arthur knew exactly where he was and had every intention of staying there.

Distracted by the recent news, he didn't see her coming. Wearing lime-green trainers and a fluffy yellow coat, Daff darted towards him like a giant canary. Arthur steadied himself.

When she had first turned up a few weeks earlier, blind to Arthur's frostiness she proudly announced she was sixty-eight and an amateur historian looking for a fresh start, preferably with a good-looking man. With a flagrant wink, she'd suggested he join her for a cuppa. Arthur declined the brazen invitation, claiming he couldn't leave his post.

"I'll cover," Young Gerald had offered, emerging from Medieval Gauntlets en-route to Mesozoic Fish Fossils.

Instinctively, Arthur took a comforting side-step towards the pillar.

"What's that?" asked Daff.

"A pillar," replied Arthur.
"What's its significance?"
"We're not sure, but it's very important."
"Why?"
Arthur couldn't answer.

The following week she arrived proffering one of two polystyrene cups.
"You can't bring hot drinks in here," Arthur admonished, regarding the cups as if they were about to detonate.
"Why not?" shrugged Daff, holding one out until he took it.
"It could damage the exhibits."
"What, this old thing?" She stepped dangerously close to Arthur's charge, peering at the markings. "Snakes are a symbol of change, you know. Shedding their skin signifies new beginnings, like a rebirth."
Arthur harrumphed. Another one on about change.
"The old skin represents whatever isn't working in your life. That's why it withers away." She took a sip of her tea, leaning in even closer. "The snakes are blind for a while because the old skin covers their eyes but, when it sheds, everything becomes clear again." She replaced the lid on her cup and stepped back.
Arthur relaxed, putting his cup to his lips.
"And sex of course! The Ancient Greeks believed they appear if you're struggling with carnal longings."
Arthur swallowed his tea in a scalding gulp.

That evening, Arthur couldn't concentrate on his jigsaw: that woman was getting under his skin. However, when she next bustled in, his lips formed an involuntary smile.
"Aye-aye," said Young Gerald. "Your lady friend's arrived."
Arthur pulled his brows into a frown.
"Hello Arthur," she said, offering him a Tupperware container. "I had a bit of shepherd's pie left over."
"But Thursday's my shepherd's pie night."
"Time to live a little, lovey."

"Let me put that in the fridge," offered Young Gerald.

"About this pillar," began Daff. "I've been doing some research. It's not Egyptian – lack of flora. Definitely not Persian – they liked a well-hung centaur, but then don't we all? I reckon it's Roman. Entwined snakes are medical. I wrote the word down." Retrieving a piece of paper from her bag she thrust it at Arthur. "Caduceus. Healing. See?"

With each visit, Daff regaled him with her life story, and even though some of her revelations were rather avant-garde, he began to enjoy listening to her, which was why today's news was even more devastating.

"What on earth's the matter?" asked Daff.

"Lump," he managed to say. "It's over."

Putting the cups on the floor, Daff wrapped her arms around him like a yellow-winged angel, surprising Arthur with how comforting it felt.

"Surely there's something they can do?" she whispered, finally releasing him.

"There's nothing anyone can do."

"When did you find out?"

"This morning."

"And you came to work?"

"That's where I found out. She just turned up and told me."

"Who?" asked Daff.

"The woman from the council."

"Why is a woman from the council telling you about a lump?"

"Not a lump. LUMP. The Little-Underton Museum of Peculiarities."

He'd pleaded to keep his job, offered to do it alone when Young Gerald left, but the woman had shaken her head.

"The museum won't be here," she'd informed him. "It's closing."

He didn't hear the rest – something about footfall, overheads, roof repairs.

"You bloody idiot!" Daff snapped. "I thought you were dying!"

"I feel as though I am. What will I do? This is my life."

"Don't be ridiculous. There's a whole world out there."

"Out there?" Arthur eyed the door with alarm.

"You need to let this go." She waved her yellow arm around. "Standing here day in, day out isn't a life. Time to move on. Try something new. Make some friends."

Tracing his finger down the snakes' outlines, Arthur pondered. Since being cuckolded, his life had been one of deliberate solitude; how could he change now?

"It's too late."

"It's never too late," replied Daff. "Bring your tea. Let's sit in the sunshine. Get a bit of warmth on our old bones."

That night, the back of Arthur's neck felt unusually sore. Twisting around, he peered in the mirror and noticed he was rather sunburned. In fact, the skin was already beginning to peel.

Sally lives not far from the sea in Bournemouth, Dorset. She has been published online, in literary publications and included in several anthologies. A keen short story and flash fiction writer, she has won various competitions, including Flash 500 and West Word historical flash, with her proudest achievement being the Dorset Award as highest placed local author in the 2024 Bridport Prize. She has full-length stories published by Hysteria, Pulp Fictional, Michael Terrance Publishers and Hammond House. Sally is aiming to complete a Novella-in-Flash and her long neglected novel now that she has semi-retired from the world of teaching, as well as hosting flash fiction and short story workshops.

www.facebook.com/sallywritesstories/

Consumed

Sarah Breen

"If you stay here, you will die."

That's not true. I have supplies: food, shelter, water, medicine. What else do I need? I have enough for weeks, maybe a month. My body will weaken, but I can stay. I can wait for a rescue.

"The grass will swallow you," she says. She watches me, her eyes flicking between me, my shuttle, and the branches that sway above us.

I thought that it would be quiet here in the forest. But there is always movement. I hear birds, but I do not see them. Something is chirping, or is it scratching?

There is no life on the ground. I keep my food sealed in the hold even though I haven't seen any insects.

The smells of wet earth and organic decay are so heavy I sense them brushing against my skin. Something is blooming; the sweetness collects in my throat.

The girl squints up at the trees and then checks the display of the metal monitor attached to her wrist.

"Why should I trust you?" I ask, my voice as hard as the lump of panic swelling beneath my rib cage.

Her lips twitch into a semblance of a smile but her eyes remain unfeeling.

"Because you will be bones in a week. Stay here if you like. Your supplies will last, but you won't."

I don't move. Her hands and face are clean even though her clothes look as if they are about to grow roots of their own. Her stained, grey trousers are aged and look like they were made for a large man, not the whip of a girl before me. But she moves with ease, as if this is a part of her, like hair or teeth. Or claws.

"I cannot leave," I hear myself say. It is the first time I've spoken these words aloud. "My team is coming for me. They are expecting me."

"Then they should expect a corpse. You've been here for one, one and a half cycles at most. First, your skin will itch. Soon your eyes will flow, followed quickly by your nose. Your fingernails will start to sting at the roots."

"Is it poison?" I ask.

"No. You are the poison."

I blink and dig my heels into the soft soil to stop my knees from shaking.

"We. Us. We are the infection. The cells are rushing to the wound, to the irritation on the surface. This forest, this land, it breaks you down until you are components to be used, absorbed."

"Natural decomposition. I've heard of it. Some plants are..."

"This is not natural," she interrupts. "It is accelerated, exponentially faster."

Above us, the leaves shuffle against one another. To my right, a branch tips toward me, its smooth bark shimmering iridescent like an oil slick. Long, thin leaves reach out, shifting color in the dappled light, their edges like bird feathers, like finger bones.

"Pack your things and put this on."

I look down at her hand. A swath of filmy cloth, gray like ash, flows over the edge of a thin, waterproof satchel.

"I'm not going with you," I say, even as I reach for the bag.

If I leave, they may never find me. But I know that if I send her away, I may never find her again or survive if half of what she is telling me is true.

I pack my things. When I drop my log book and my physical mementos into its shadowy recesses, a puff of dust (or is it pollen?) is displaced. I add protein rations and two vials of purified water, wondering if I will regret the extra weight. She tells me to leave them, that she will not poison me. Regardless, I keep one of each. I'm tempted to argue with her for more, but she won and we both know it. If she were to kill me, she would have done it here, alone, on the floor of the forest on this forgotten planet.

I follow her instructions and cover my head so my hair will not touch the branches. I don't understand, but I don't argue. I tug at the gloves, struggling to fit my sweaty fingers into their snug confines. They are too small, and my heartbeat pulses in my fingertips. My neck is tacky with sweat,, and I fight the instinct to rip off these suffocating layers so I can breathe.

As I open my mouth to ask why this is necessary, she tips her head toward a massive tree. Between roots as thick as a man's leg, water has collected in a narrow hollow.

Leaning over, careful as to not step against the water's rim, she spits, her saliva stretching until it slips into the center of the puddle.

At first, nothing happens. In the span of a breath, the water begins to bubble. Green tendrils snake in from the pool's edges, perfect in their symmetry and breathtaking in their speed. They meet in the center and dart downward toward the intruder.

I cannot breathe.

"It eats you alive," she says, her voice flat. "Healing? Dying? It doesn't matter."

"But I can escape it."

She looks at me.

"You've never been hunted before, have you?"

When I don't answer, she pivots to a narrow gap between two blackened trunks. There is no path. She moves among the foliage quietly, as if she were a ghost, as if she had never passed through here before. I can't see any footsteps or other evidence from when she arrived, silver-eyed and silent, a portent of a ravenous ecology.

"Stay close," she says. And then we are moving.

Sarah Breen lives in Berlin, Germany. She is happiest curled up on her sofa with a fantasy or YA novel or texting bad jokes and cute animal videos to her family in America. Her writing spans several genres, including romance, urban fantasy, science fiction, and general fiction. She was shortlisted in the short story category for Hysteria 10.

linkedin.com/in/breensarah/

Reaching Home

Stephanie Percival

Kyle peers round the edge of the gate, surveying the wasteland before him. He tries to think like his big brother taught him. Daniel is in the army, went to Afghanistan.

A haze of dust hovers low over the ground. The summer's been so hot everything is dried, the grass parched brown. Kyle squints as light shimmers off a wrecked car.

Further away he sees the place he needs to reach. The middle of the rec, where an ancient tree grows. The main trunk is black and scarred from a lightning strike. Surviving branches are gnarled. A few scant leaves cling but are shrivelled and rusted. Two captives are already imprisoned near the tree, rattling the bars of their cage. Kyle watches the bulky figure of the enemy lurking nearby, prowling around searching him out. The enemy sniffs the air, nostrils flared. Kyle retreats behind the barrier. How can he get over there, without being caught? 'Think like a soldier. Objective. Evaluate. Contingency. Execute...'

He's already negotiated piles of rubble, overflowing dustbins. To his left there are bushes which would conceal him, but that's close to the pond; muddy edges fissured from the heat. A pool of oily water winks in the centre where something skulks, partially submerged. Waiting. On the right there's a row of three scrawny trees which won't provide much cover. Sharp little shadows splay beneath each one. Another option is along the ridge, circling the rec. The slant of sun casts it into dark shadow. Who knows what danger lies there? Sweat seeps down Kyle's face.

Daniel peers round the edge of what once was a door; now shattered planks. He surveys the wasteland of the street. Smells of oil and burning fill the air; seeping into him, mingling with his own unwashed stench. His fatigues, dusted and dirty, soggy with sweat.

A haze of dust hovers low over the ground. The day's too hot as usual, everything dried and parched. Daniel squints as light shimmers off wrecked cars lining the street. Abandoned houses crumble on either side, exposing once lived in rooms. A drape, an armchair, a lampshade, all grey with dust as though relics from a forgotten time. Reminders that people used to live ordinary lives here; places where families used to jostle, children used to play. Daniel thinks of his young brother, Kyle, and smiles; imagines him running on the rec with his mates. Remembers the innocence and freedom of days when he'd run and played with them too. The thought lightens the tension in his shoulders, the weight of the gun he carries. He shakes his head, clearing his thoughts. He needs to focus.

Further away he's identified the place he must reach. The husk of a house, where he'll be safe. The ground between him and there is riddled with traps. Mines dotted; enemy soldiers hidden ready to pounce. He can make out the tops of two helmets, those of his comrades, dusty beetle backs scurrying behind a tumbled wall. They're nearer to the house, but with a similar treacherous path to take before they can reach safety.

A bird glides overhead, a wide-winged silhouette against the sun, which dazzles when Daniel looks up. He blinks trying to rid his vision of the sunspots blinding him.

He makes his decision to go. 'Three, two, one...' He moves from his hiding place, crouched over, treading carefully, to avoid leaving a telltale trail of dust. Then he runs, scrambles to the old house, darts in, flops down. Letting out a deep breath, he has a moment to pause, thinks of his home in England. So far away and so different from this world. He smiles, thinking of Kyle again; a skinny, plucky kid, who worships Daniel. Wants to be just like him. He'll see him soon, if he survives this tour of duty. Daniel leans back against the crumbling wall, closes his eyes and daydreams. A fleeting gust of wind, triggers a waft of dust. Daniel suppresses a cough, his smile fading. Happy recollections clouded by the knowledge that here, freedom and innocence have been lost.

Kyle gets to his hands and knees, stubby grass rasping against his shins. He runs crouched over, scrambles to the first tree and stands up. The trunk is skinny, but Kyle is skinny too, his blue T-shirt merges with the patch of blue-green shade beneath the tree. As the enemy moves further away, Kyle tiptoes down the row of trees... Three, two, one... He is so close now. He leans against the final tree trunk, takes a deep breath, preparing to run.

The enemy is making another sweep this way so Kyle presses into the tree and stands motionless. After a minute of holding his breath, he's dizzy. But he's not been spotted. Now's his chance.

He sprints towards the gnarled tree. His legs spinning as fast as they can. The captives are yelling at him, "Watch out! Watch out!"

Kyle reaches for the trunk of the tree. Just as he lunges for it and shouts, "Home!" the enemy reaches out and grabs him, wrestling Kyle to the ground.

"Got you!"

"No, you didn't!" Kyle yells back.

"Did, did, did..." Daniel repeats, tickling him, until Kyle is squealing, "Okay, Okay, I give in."

Daniel pulls off the upturned shopping trolley caging Kyle's two mates and says, "Not bad. I'll make soldiers of you yet."

They share a bottle of warm cola, and then sit in the sun. Daniel sits a little way a way, his back towards them. He's very still, staring into space. A bird circles high above, just a black shape gliding in the expanse of sky. Kyle watches Daniel, wonders what he's thinking. But the motionless, broad back of his brother is like a sign saying, 'Do not disturb.'

Kyle lies back on the ground. Feels the heat of the earth beneath his shoulders, watches white clouds slip across a perfect blue sky, smiles. Anticipating the day he'll be a real soldier.

Stephanie's writing journey began in 2004, when she was shortlisted for the BBC End of Story Competition. Since then, she's continued to learn her craft. She's realised she'll never make a living from writing but gets a buzz from seeing her work in print. In 2011, she self-published a novel, 'The Memory of Wood.' This is a psychological mystery, set in her home county of Northamptonshire. Her writing explores different genres and themes. She writes flash, short, long fiction and poetry and enjoys experimenting with form and style. She's had work published in anthologies and on-line and has been short and long-listed. Occasionally, she wins! Last year, Stephanie published a collection of these stories, called 'How to Catch and Keep a Kiss.'

www.stephaniepercival.com

WHEN HARRY MET SALLY

Stephen Welsh

Not today. No. Not today. But the day will come, and I will know that my time is limited. But today I sit in my motorised wheelchair by my mother's bedside. And she clings to my hand tightly. So very tightly.

'I wanted to die after you,' she said, sweating with the pain.

'It's me who should look after you, not some useless care home. And don't you tell anyone about that debit card. Don't, do you hear me?'

She's looked after me these last 40 years. Me, this 90kg mass of limited mobility. I have sensations in my body, and I can move my right hand. I cannot speak, but my laptop can. It takes me half an hour to write a sentence with my right hand and save it to my 'stock phrases'. All twelve of them.

'I said do you hear me?'

I press the mouse pad.

Stock Phrase #1

'Yes'.

And now she faces what she has most dreaded. Her death before mine.

'It's just not fucking fair,' she says and dies, not peacefully, but with rage.

Two years later

What is it that makes me a man? I can shit and piss and my adult nappy takes the strain, but doing things, the way in which most men express themselves, I cannot do. What then, makes me a man?

'Mr Taggert?' This care worker is new. I see first her purple hair and the tattoos on her neck and bare arms.

'Fancy going for a walk?'

Outside my bedroom, the sun is shining. I pause and consider, then press 'yes' and we're off. As soon as she's out of the care home she inserts a ring in her nose and large spangled earrings in her ear lobes. She takes a furtive glance at the office, pulls out a cigarette and lights up. We're on a tarmacked pathway in the park and the wind blows on my face and through my hair.

'My name's Sally,' she says. 'What's yours?'

Stock phrase #6.

'My name's Harry.'

I smile, but she doesn't recognise the pairing of our names with Meg Ryan and Billy Crystal. In the corner of my eye, I see a young man approaching fast on his electric scooter, head down looking at his mobile. He slams into my wheelchair and falls off. Getting up he says,

'You fucker.'

And Sally slaps his face. I can see the red marks of her fingers on his cheek.

'Speak nicely, you little twat.'

He throws a fist at her head. She dodges. I've seen the move in boxing matches on the TV. She shifts her balance, steps to his side and with impressive speed, punches the side of his head. He drops like a stone.

'He'll live,' she says, and we motor on. I have a boxer for a care worker! Back in my room, for the first time in decades, I write a new stock phrase.

Stock phrase #13

What the fuck.

A week later

We watch 'When Harry met Sally' on Netflix. The film finishes and she wipes her eyes and says,

'So they make it in the end? That's Hollywood, not real life. Not mine.'

A month later

'Do you fancy having your hair dyed purple?'

Stock phrase #12.

'That would be very nice. Thank you.'

Three months later

Sally doesn't look me in the eye. She's pacing around my room, tidying up what she's already tidied up. Then she looks at me.

'Don't think I'm a weirdo, but,' and she pauses, 'Would you like sex with me?'

A very long pause.

Stock phrase #12.

'That would be very nice. Thank you.'

She does what she needs to do, turns and sits on me. It's over pretty soon.

What is it that makes me a man? I get angry but cannot express it. I cry at some of the films I watch. I listen to people talking but cannot take part in their conversation. Sitting in a wheelchair, shitting and pissing my pants, being hoisted by a sling into the shower, having my arse wiped yet again. What is it that makes me a man?

I have some new stock phrases.

'Harry,' says Sally, 'Fancy a quickie?'

Stock phrase #56.

'Not half.'

We're going for it, and in honour of our favourite film, I press Yes, Yes, Yes over and over again. Sally collapses laughing. It's all rather messy and she hoists me, giggling, into the shower.

Some months later

I awake, and I feel a pull inside me, something like the moon pulling the tide. It won't be today, but it will be soon, and my ending will be painful. The debit card rests in a slit inside my left armrest. A month before she died, my mother and I confirmed all the details for my pre-paid appointment in Switzerland, date pending. Sally breezes into the room. Straight away, she knows something's up. I've already written the stock phrase.

'Sally. Will you drive me to Switzerland?'

Two weeks later

Sally straps me and my chair into the back of the wheelchair accessible van. She booked the ferry, hired the van. She's dyed her hair bright yellow for the occasion and mine a bright red.

'One for the road?' she says.

Stock phrase #101

'I thought you'd never ask.'

Three days later

My right finger hovers above the plastic red button. Sally clings to my left hand, tightly, so very tightly.

'Harry. We can still go back. There'll be help with the pain. And I'll be there for you.'

What is it that makes me a man? I look into Sally's eyes and sense, right there and then, that I no longer have to ask the question. And I realise too, for the first time in my life, that I can make a choice other than what I'm going to have for breakfast.

'Harry. Shall we go back?'

Stock phrase #12

'That would be very nice. Thank you.'

Stephen Welsh was brought up in Jarrow on the banks of the River Tyne. He began writing when he was 9 years old, sitting by himself at night in the kitchen, a flickering strip light above him, enjoying the feel of a blank page and a fountain pen in his hand. He's written six novels (unpublished). In 2020 he won the Black Spring Press Group's Crime Fiction competition with his book 'Expiation.'

He lives in the South Pennines and is a member of Wednesday Writers, a fortnightly writing group that meets in the nearby town of Todmorden. The group members write a short story or poem to a theme pulled out of a hat and then read it aloud at the next meeting. He is also one of a group of four writers who run a monthly spoken word Open Mic called Gobshite.

www.ingramcontent.com/pod-product-compliance
Lightning Source LLC
Chambersburg PA
CBHW060342080526
44584CB00013B/875